DUAL EXPOSURE

POEMS BY
BARBARA SAXTON

BLUE LIGHT PRESS

DUAL EXPOSURE

Copyright 2015 By Barbara Saxton

BOOK DESIGN
Melanie Gendron

ISBN: 978-1-4218-3733-8

1ST WORLD LIBRARY
PO Box 2211
Fairfield, Iowa 52556
www.1stworldpublishing.com

BLUE LIGHT PRESS
www.bluelightpress.com
Email: bluelightpress@aol.com

Publication Acknowledgements

Thank you to the editors who have published my works, sometimes in earlier versions.

Shared Light (The Willow Glen Poetry Project), Volume One, 2011: "Bloodline" (formerly titled "Sisterhood Is Powerful)

No Ordinary Language (The Willow Glen Poetry Project), Volume Two, 2013: "Matching Dresses" and "Grace under Pressure"

The Haight Ashbury Literary Journal, Volume 31, Number 1, 2014: "Chanticleer"

My Kitchen Table, Summer 2014 issue: "Plum Worship"

Uncharted Frontier Ezine, Sept. 2013 issue: "Plum Worship"

River of Earth and Sky: Poems for the Twenty-First Century, Anthology of Poetry published by Blue Light Press, 2015: "Dual Exposure" and "Matching Dresses"

Contents

Dual Exposure..1

Hangover Sundays...2

Lightning Rod...3

Memorial Days...5

Matching Dresses..6

Cherry Vanilla Evening..8

Boxing Day...10

Chanticleer..11

Consigning Mother's Ring...12

Bloodline..13

All Ears...15

The Night I Called His Wife..16

Asian Joy Ride...17

Perigee...19

Aikido...21

Root Canal...23

In Marjorie's Garden...24

Grace under Pressure...25

Plum Worship...27

Occupy...28

Sound Tracks...30

For Owen...31

Hallmark This!...32

About the Author...33

Dual Exposure

Deposited on a ragged stone wall,
elastic grin and wide-stretched arms
challenging Niagara's full force, a four year old girl
flaunts the warrior's stance
and level gaze of some long-forgotten race,
rewarding parents who posed her in the foreground of danger
with their precious souvenir.

A half-century later, picture a grown woman's spine,
trapped immobile in a hospital's imaging submarine.
Depth charges boom the length of her once-fluid torso
as she dreams of out-dancing sciatica's eddies,
then curtsies to pain, her perpetual partner,
who drowns out all music in the background of bliss.

Put down your camera.
This vista's off limits.

Hangover Sundays

Had I hatched from some idyllic nest,
where sitcom sires returned each night
to barf back remnants of their days,
my childhood home might not have been
that forest of unruly caws and drunken brawls
preceding sullen, scary silences, the watchful eye
of booze-filled hurricanes making landfall
on our heads when least expected.

Some parts of me do come from Daddy,
prodigious elm cut down too late,
sarcastic wit the sharpened saw.
World wariness, a manic side.
A voice to sing,
and words that sting.

From Mom, I got the urge to be in charge
with insufficient power to do it.
Bitter sap whose pressure builds
until the family trunk nearly explodes,
taking our whole damn tree with it.

For years, I flew from church to church,
looking for an oaken pew that bore my name,
and under it, a survivor's soul
to help me through another season.

Lightning Rod

Your first light from her eyes.
Your first mission to spare her
the pains of her world. Your head
smooth and bald, you danced drugged
down the slippery birth canal.
Perfect baby: you cooed,
smiled and whistled before you were ready.

Whenever he came after her,
the light drew you, her child,
to her side of each battle.
Sweet avenging angel, you were bred
to take blows for her sake,
your dark bruises obscured
by loose clothing and pride.

Barely fifteen, and once again lured
by the light, you stumbled down
a four a.m. hallway to find her sprawled,
cold and motionless, on the bathroom floor.
Only light knows what made you wake up,
how you managed to dial 911, murmuring: *We need help.*
My mom's swallowed some pills...

Fast forward to lifting a different phone
from its cradle, hearing him try to break her door
down with a hammer. You fumble for car keys,
drive through rain-filled streets, barge past him,
get her out.

Much later, you'd hold her left hand
while her right signed the papers
to end fifty years
of miserable marriage.

Light urges our wombs
to fill with sweet life, ignoring the terror
of passing on sorrowful genes.
Sometimes, though, we seek peace
filled only by darkness.

Memorial Days

It's been one hundred years
since my father was born,
and in one form or another,
inhabited the earth.

Once again, I embark
on my tired pilgrimage
to a windswept mound in Colma,
where we have it on faith
his ashes now rest,
under neatly mown grass
and a tersely-carved stone.

On my last visit, I stole a drooping daisy
from a stranger's plot next door
and laid it on my father's grave. Before I left, I watered both
with a disappointed daughter's
brackish tears.

Matching Dresses

On the path from uncertainty
to my neighborhood Safeway, I braked
for a mother and daughter
who sashayed through the crosswalk
in matching magenta-striped dresses.
Half a century before, other drivers had halted
while my mother and I proudly strolled hand
in hand across elm-shaded streets, modeling
brand new yellow seersucker shirtwaists.

Thanks to the Depression, and marriage
to a man who insisted we women were
No good at anything, my mother never drove;
so we walked, mismatched twins,
our twined fingers faintly scented
by the Aquamarine she applied every night
before bed. In summer, our white strappy
sandals clip-clopped unison rhythms
over the near-molten sidewalks. In winter,
four rubber galoshes pounded parallel
purposeful tracks in the snow.

Those sounds, scents, impressions
have since disappeared, but this daughter's strong legs,
toughened by urban journeys, persist
with the sense that together we'd face
any terrors the streets held in store. Even now,
while navigating uncharted territories, I sometimes
still reach for her hand.

As I watched that magenta-clad duo,
I longed to shout out: *Sweet Girl, hold on tight!*
That warmth and connection cannot
last forever. But instead, I kept
to my path, a little less eager to arrive
somewhere no one would know me.

Cherry Vanilla Evening

The extra long chains on my neighbor's
tall swings heaved us into the late summer sky.
We pointed audacious bare toes
at the evening's first stars, pretending it wasn't yet time
to race home on our beaten-up bikes, tanned forearms
glistening in topaz half-darkness.

A slammed screen door away, my favorite bowl
of *Cherry Vanilla* awaited me. I saw myself perched
on the hassock cross-legged in our darkening den,
spooning in sweetness, while Perry Como crooned
on TV.

But, as I lay down my bike,
I saw a tell-tale red speck
float above the back yard. A firefly, perhaps,
flight trajectory skewed? *Who are you kidding?*
I asked, parental-angst radar set on full alert.

First, sour cigarette smoke.
Then, I took in the whole package:
my mommy sprawled on a chaise lounge,
wearing only her nightgown, a beer can
in one hand, unfiltered Phillip Morris
in the other.

Hi Barbie, her Schlitz-y voice slurred.
Glad you're home.

Newly mown grass prickling legs
that had recently swung free, I sat by her side,
imaginary pencil and pad ready, striking
my usual fake-concerned pose.

Her self-absorbed narrative droned
on and on. I hummed and I clucked
at all the right intervals, while innocence puddled
like melted ice cream
round my eight-year-old feet.

Boxing Day

Just when it seemed safe,
another one's in the bag!
Christmas creeps from his corner
coated in red and green crumbs
to land yet another
sucker punch to the gut.

In the midst of this mess
of cleaved wrappings, parched needles
and pale half-licked canes, I croon
to the bittersweet carols of memory--
Mom's face and her voice.

Chanticleer

Last night at Saint Ignatius Church,
the house lights dimmed
and plainsong chant
danced down
from apse to nave.

Votives winked in dim recesses
as lights from passing cars on Fulton
gifted furtive glimpse of stained glass
wonders far above.

I glanced up there for you,
and mouthed my usual vow
to mine enough of all this beauty
for the two of us, then waited
for my killjoy mind to argue

She can't hear you.

And even if she could,
she'd sense it all eternally,
when all you have is this
one magic night.

Consigning Mother's Ring

It shouldn't have been willed to me.
I'm not an emerald and baguette diamond girl.
I'm set in steel, not platinum.

Technically, it's called a *dinner ring*,
but we all knew it as a form
of circular apology
for cocktail hour abuse.
Advance payment, if you will,
for dessert wines
served up with purple bruises.

For twenty-three long years,
I kept it tucked away
in an emotionally
distant drawer.

But Sally's house needs a new roof,
and something good should finally come
of all that ostentatious glinting.

Before leaving the consignment store,
I kissed those gems that once adorned
a hand now far beyond
her daughter's loving grasp.

Bloodline

Another 3 AM call.
All I hear is your breathing.
I breathe back, playing chicken,
back and forth, each of us hoping
the other hangs up first;
lungs pulsing, hearts beating,
through our one open bloodline.

I wait, reliving a time long ago
when our seven- and twelve-year-old selves
invaded that bakery, demanding donuts in character,
my Tweety to your Sylvester:

Cweem-filled gwazed,
pweety pweeze.
Stop dat, you mean ole puddy tat!

Laughing too hard to eat,
nearly peeing our pants, we ran
down those hot Cleveland streets, stopping
just out of range, gasping and grasping
in silly solidarity.

I'd never had so much fun,
so next time you appeared
at the door to my cage, inviting me out,
I let down my guard, flapping eagerly to you,
only to feel those familiar claws digging deep
in my wings, your sharp jealous teeth
clamping my tail feathers.

Did you call tonight wondering
which sister would answer?
Dumb, gullible Tweety,
or that pissed-off storekeeper, warning you
to take your business elsewhere?

But it's late, and now I'm too tired
for games. My cage door is locked tight,
but I feel you out there, breathing and waiting.
I'm seven again, nesting in a dark corner,
vowing not to give in to our god-damned
depweshun.

All Ears

Squinting into the midsummer sun,
hair damp, vaguely swampy,
from our swimming hole sojourn, we stopped
at the same roadside stand where the owner
had promised to save us four ears
of his prize-winning corn.

It was well after six. I was sure
the best part of our dinner was already sold
to ladies en route to their bingo in Dalton.
But my wise sister insisted this farmer,
Southern wit and beer belly both straining
what buttons remained on a sweat-stained
plaid shirt, would honor the four-word reminder
he'd scrawled on his dirty white card.

And he did,
even adding, like some outsize elf,
a bonus fifth ear,
without charging us more.

Where I come from, promises are as fickle
as breezes that ruffle your tall Georgia pines,
then hasten to tickle the boughs of red maples.
In a week, I'd fly back
to that insincere world.

When aliens come, may they unearth
and savor huge kernels of our sweet,
yet elusive, integrity.

The Night I Called His Wife

Coming to terms with personal shadows,
side-stepping *pretty,*
embracing the muck. Trample on grammar
and syntax. Go everywhere
you don't want to look. So drunk one night,
I crank-called his wife,
to share lies we were living.

The press of his hand
on the back of my new silky dress
as we whirl round the floor.
The shy way he asks for my help
choosing kids' birthday presents.
In moments of passion, he never cries out
her name. But boy how he craves
my tuna casserole.

What Greek sin of pride
made me blurt out my name?
Thanks to Star-69, she called back right away
to cry and beseech me to leave her alone.
Small comfort, this suffering out loud.

Afterward, the room reeked
of my carrion lust for another woman's
poor property.

Asian Joy **Ride**

Under cover of midnight, like satay dipped
in slick peanut sauce, the *Asian Joy* slid
into Singapore Strait.
Every light on the shore twinkled promise
of clean sheets, hot showers, and porcelain cups
of strong English tea.

After seven nights in a cramped cargo hold,
rocked to uneasy sleep by sea swells and snores
of old Chinese men on nearby creaky cots, I yearned
for dawn light brighter than the few rays
that managed to shine through cracks
in the floor above deck. No more waiting in line
for Cook's foul-smelling *jook*, sparsely sprinkled
with dry, rancid shrimp.

But these buoyant thoughts sank
when a rude British sailor in neatly-creased shorts
and blinding-white socks flung a flimsy rope ladder
down one side of the ship. *Welcome to Singapore*, he sneered,
inviting us to descend undulating wet rungs, then leap
across three feet of churning black sea to bumboats
that bobbed wildly in the waves far below.

Catapult to old age, or share the weird fate
of female ghosts in that Japanese film
we watched on the rear deck a few nights before?
Robes a-flutter, their black eyebrows arched high
on creamy broad foreheads, these girls quickly dispersed
in South China Sea mist when a sudden gust
blew our cheap screen overboard.

First class passengers high above
watched us jump, perhaps mistaking
the oddly-shaped lumps for their luggage. Upon landing,
I blamed my strange trembling voice
on the boat's noisy motor.

The distance of years
makes it harder than ever
to read the fine print
on our lives' one-way tickets.

Perigee

It wasn't an official date. He never asked
if I'd be free to see his super-sized arrival,
heralded in my morning paper
next to an article on fly-fishing
therapy for veterans.

Still, evening found me bravely biking
through pre-dusk traffic, hoping to arrive in time
at our crude rendezvous: an overpass
adorned with windswept wrappers,
wads of well-loved gum, and empty Red Bull cans,
set to the charming soundtrack of nonstop
vehicular caterwauling.

His warm-up act of crimson lava
snaked down the western hills, subsiding
to warm alpenglow on the horizon. A sudden chill
invaded my thin jacket as I paced the dirty sidewalk,
squinting through a chain link fence for signs
of my bridegroom's arrival.

Being jilted, even at unlikely altars,
always stings. My foot was poised
to flip the kickstand up and leave,
when a narrow slice of gray forehead
bulged against the eastern hills. Then, the rest
of my beloved's pockmarked face appeared,
borrowing peach palettes from sister Sunset's wardrobe.
He blushed at my attention, as if unused to filling
such enormous chunks of sky.

Smug scientists try to explain
why moons sometimes seem over-full.
We poets may be more impressed
by perigee's effects than curious
about its cause.

Afterward, I biked home, gesturing wildly
to motorists immune to such miracle moons.
The night breeze knit my words
to ancient melodies that float on velvet chords
and ricochet off lighted picture windows.

Aikido

Just a part of the enormity of wrong
in our relationship, martial arts proved a deal-breaker
when he appeared to love wearing that white suit
and ribbed belt even more than lying
in bed next to me.

As if celebrating my new status
of *Aikido widow,* I was gifted a treatise
called *Centering,* unrivaled for pretension
and sheer rectangular smugness.
Before shoving it under the mental mat
I normally reserve for unsolicited issues
of *Watchtower,* one day I actually started to read it,
more than ever lamenting my lack of a *center.*
I'm all edges and angles
that furiously compete for my body's
unfocused attention.

For months, I aimed at higher levels
of *centeredness,* aware that my efforts
were at fatal odds with the book's dire
admonition *not to try.* Every somersault I faked,
every failure to tuck in a jutting-out chin
to my soon-to-be broken neck, every flip
that crumpled my poor body sideways
like a heap of soiled laundry, all left me hurtling
light-speed *toward,* not away from,
the land of the cock-eyed and skewed.

I mean, if the gods created us humans
to ratchet through space in this manner,
why couldn't we keep more of our
ancestors' padding?

Meanwhile, down at the *dojo,*
match after mismatch, I strove
to ignore now-familiar desires to strike
the first punch (or worse yet,
annihilate) my would-be attackers.
More yin and less yang, our *Sensei* intoned.
Turn their force against them! Truth be told,
in my pseudo-martial encounters, it was
Aikido itself that whizzed past both of my shoulders
smack into the wall, dead-centered in my life's
rear-view mirror.

Sir Centered and Dame Scattered
soon headed in equal and opposite directions.
But my black belt in honesty
would only be earned about thirty years later,
when I finally donated that dastardly book
to Goodwill.

Root Canal

Snip. Gouge.
Dry the dead canal.
Kill pain. Chop limb:
the tree survives.

Last night I woke
to the dream knock of intruders,
storming my brain's gate
through a bicuspid's open portal.

My index finger grazed
sponge enamel: a throbbing bath toy
one might pinch and yank out
of its tub of molten pain

Dental Mercy Goddess,
focus your magical scope
on misery's epicenter.
extract the pesky nerve!

I leave with nothing floating
in a vial that might have joined
my growing trophy shelf
of warrior memories.

In Marjorie's Garden

Poetry is an open messenger for your soul's wisdom. —Diane Frank

Lounging awhile in her garden of pot,
I decode cryptic crosswords, weed out
random thoughts, high-five waxy green
pointed leaves, and sniff dewy residue
of heady night jasmine, mixed with cannabis'
signature *Eau de Skunk.*

How smoothly the sculpted owl's head
rotates on his pock-marked grey granite slab,
while his driftwood friend morphs
into a fearsome bottom feeder,
trolling the pebble moat for stray
remnants of plankton.

Meanwhile, on their rosemary cloud,
cement-shawled Madonna and her cross-legged Buddha
exchange repressed, holy glances. Above their bowed heads,
crimson hollyhock mouths trumpet tunes
with the brass angel twins, tacked captive and mute
on the far western wall.

Who could object to remaining, marooned,
in this magical garden? Her sundial points to *now,*
while her green grapevine helix
rocks me in eternal embrace.

If sorrow exists in Marjorie's Garden,
it can only be found in my urge
to depart.

Grace under Pressure

To be honest, I thought her words would galumph
down the page the same way
her gargantuan feet follow rhythms
that no one else seems to hear. I was sure all her lines
would fold awkwardly back on themselves,
like her five-foot-ten frame sometimes bends
almost double, while she stares
so intently at shoes just ahead.

I berated Erato,
who made me reveal
our shared love of poetry.
I mouthed thanks to Terpsichore
each time I escaped the firm grasp
of her paw.

For months, I felt safe
from that *self-published book*
she continually mentioned.
Then, one fateful Friday, a thin volume
was pressed in my hand!
They cost me three bucks, she intoned,
so I conjured a five, murmuring,
Thanks…Keep the change.

Who knew such a simple transaction
would dispel a wealth
of mean misconceptions?

Her verse the flip side
of her frame's lumpish movements,
her images crisp and concise
as her dance steps
were gangling and gauche.

On each page, maladroit melted
into dexterity. The same soulful music
her clown feet desecrated, frolicked and waltzed
on the spring-loaded floor
of her ballroom of words.

Plum Worship

I lurk in my yard, snapping pictures
of plums which will help me recall
how those plump purple beauties
bent down the green branches,
before birds, squirrels and God knows what else
come to hurry the harvest.

Soon enough, this same tree
will shrink to its wintry black spine.
In my camera's eye, it can burgeon forever
with life and free food that tastes better
for growing on one's own piece of land.

When the season's first fruit
plummets earthward, I pause to admire
its rounded warm weight in my palm,
content to imagine its sweet juice
on my tongue.

My son planted this tree.
Now, its fruit nourishes a shrine
deep in his mother's belly, once so ripe,
nearly bursting, with someone I had yet
to meet and adore.

Occupy

A magical sight in Berkeley
at dusk: two backpacking tents
chock full of balloons, suspended
in helium stasis, and floating above them,
a hand-lettered sign ostentatiously claiming
the whole evening sky
as *Our Space*.

While digesting this splendid display,
I googled my son and soon found him,
costumed in his trappings of resurrected revolution:
threadbare jeans, oily sweatshirt,
ragged beard, accessorized by bulging knapsack
and a half-collapsed tent. Looking bemused
yet determined, armed with only convictions,
he stared down two cops in full riot regalia.

At that point, I recalled his two-hours-old self:
that newborn who stared in complete disbelief
as doctors tore him from his mother's soft arms,
then swiftly wheeled her away.

How dare you? For shame!

Like the millions of poor, homeless,
damaged or sick, I was hemorrhaging,
rivers of blood draining out. Vital organs shut down
one by one, but unlike today's victims of greed
and malfeasance, my torrents were cauterized. No such luck
for those warned to disperse, or be clubbed.

How dare you? For shame!

That evening, an ABC news feature captured
a bulldozer as it consigned one of Occupy's
more fanciful sculptures to an early dumpster grave.
In the background, a lone UC worker power-washed
evidence of protest from the pristine marble steps
of Sproul Hall.

Sound Tracks

Newborn hazel eyes
alight on my face, silver lasers
radiating equal measures
of love and outrage.

How could I leave him,
freshly born, still scented
with birth fluids?

Now, it was my turn
to descend spiral tunnels, bouncing off
scarlet walls, as my mind's canoe bobbed up,
then down, blood's treacherous
crimson currents.

Rachel died like this, punished for hiding
her father's precious idols.
She named her second son
Ben of my mourning, then bled out
with the afterbirth.

I cried my son's name
as they scraped my womb clean.
Blue tears formed the oceans
he'd soon learn to cross. My fists drummed
cold steel gurney rails in rhythms apt for mimic
by his future's supple fingers.

For Owen

The softest fur
the freshest cream
the deepest well.

Love I feared
I'd lose. Contests I thought
I'd never win.

At the concert, our fingers
touched gently, then withdrew.
Gabrieli rippled on, cadences well aware
of how gestures will swing
the rope bridge of our moods.

A nightingale's song,
an opal's cool fire,
children's innocent laughter.

Worth the pain
of someday waking
beside your plump
undented pillow.

Hallmark This!

As summer's door groans shut
on September's rust-worn hinges,
timid butterflies, their unkempt wings
tattooed with amber frowns, rummage
in my ghostly garden's clearance bin.
Last-minute shoppers seeking
nature's final markdowns.

Did I mention Autumn and I
have grown more intimate? Not only
does he enter without ringing Labor Day's
annoying bell, he also spikes
my birthday punch with bursts
of gold and russet confetti.

Huddled together, we savor sunsets
that broadcast our last episodes.

Change of seasons
Change of lives
Change embraced for nothing more
than its older, colder
stronger self.

Card message inside:
I'm still here.

ABOUT THE AUTHOR

Dual Exposure is Barbara Saxton's first book of poetry. Since emigrating to the San Francisco Bay Area from Ohio in the late 60's, she earned a B.A. in Asian Studies from the University of California (Santa Barbara), lived and traveled in Hong Kong and other areas of Asia, worked too many years in the financial services industry, married and raised two wonderful sons, and eventually transformed herself into a middle and high school English teacher. Although she has been a writer for as long as she can remember, it was only after entering the teaching profession (and beginning a long and fruitful association with Diane Frank and her ever-expanding cadre of "workshop" poets) that Barbara began to devote more time and energy to producing and refining her poetry.

In addition to Diane, Barbara would like to thank her family, friends, and fellow poets of the Willow Glen (San Jose) Poetry Project for their generous support and encouragement throughout the years.

Now retired from full-time teaching, Barbara engages in a cornucopia of activities, including classical and international folk singing and dance, world travel, gardening, hiking, substitute teaching and tutoring, as well as volunteering as a docent for her local elementary school district's garden-based ecology program. And, of course, writing: her "next book" is already under construction!

Printed in the United States of America

www.ingramcontent.com/pod-product-compliance
Lightning Source LLC
Chambersburg PA
CBHW051741040426
42447CB00008B/1244